HEALTH CARE
NEEDS
OF
A MULTI-RACIAL
SOCIETY

Authors:
Perminder (Pami) Bal S.R.N.,
        M.A. in Community and Health Ethics.
Equality Advisor
North Mersey Community Trust, Liverpool.

Gurdev S Bal B.A.
Computer Systems Manager
The University of Liverpool.

Published by Hawker Publications Ltd, London.

First Published in 1995 by
Hawker Publications Ltd
13 Park House
140 Battersea Park Road
London SW11 4NB

British Library Cataloguing in Publication Data

A Catalogue record for this book is available
from the British Library

ISBN 1-874790-23-X

Designed by Richard Souper and Gurdev Bal

Printed and bound by Joseph Ward Colour Print Ltd,
Dewsbury

CONTENTS

ABOUT THE AUTHORS

Pami is of Indian origin, born and brought up in East Africa, and has worked as a Health Care Professional in the UK for over 30 years. She has gained a reputation as an expert in Equal Opportunities, especially in the diverse Health Care needs of a multi-racial society. She is also an external verifier for City and Guilds, advising on NVQs in care.

Gurdev is of Indian origin, born and educated in India, and has worked in Higher Education in the UK for over 28 years. He regularly translates and proof reads the leaflets in Punjabi for the local community. He has reproduced the religious symbols and occasional greetings etc., in the vernacular using computer graphics.

ACKNOWLEDGEMENTS

Acknowledgements are due to many friends and colleagues who have assisted us in the production of this book. Special thanks are extended to Mr Sunder Chopra for his advice and valuable contributions.

Grateful thanks are extended to Helen Owen and the staff of the Chinese Pagoda Centre, Mangala (Mr. E. wright) from the Buddhist Centre, Rabbi M. Malits from the Hebrew Congregation, Mr. H.M. Aslam from the Friends Information Centre and Zuhoor Al-Khanjari for verification of the contents.

We are particularly indebted to our son, Jaspaul for type-setting the script.

Thanks are also extended to all family members and friends who provided photographs from their personal collections to enhance the contents of the book.

PREFACE

The main purpose of this book is to assist Care Staff to plan and deliver a high quality of care which is appropriate and relevant for the diverse needs of their clients taking into account their religious and/or cultural beliefs.

The book is divided into three sections:

SECTION I - RELIGIONS OF THE WORLD

This section explains in simple language, the main philosophy of each religion and its influence on everyday life.

SECTION II - WAY OF LIFE

This section provides information about the main groups within the community and their diverse needs.

SECTION III - OTHER USEFUL INFORMATION

This section includes other information which practitioners may find useful.

INTRODUCTION

The National Health Service (NHS) and the Community Care Reforms (CCR) of 1990 have made it explicit that health and social services should be planned and provided in a manner which takes account of the needs of the whole community. The 1991 UK Census figures confirm that 5.5 percent of the population or three million people, are from the Black and Minority Communities. Several studies have confirmed that health and social services departments have failed to provide services which are equally accessible or appropriate to meet the needs of the Black and Minority Communities.

The NHS Patients Charter 1991 has specified Nine National Charter Standards which are to be used to measure the standard of care provided for the users of services. The first and the most important standard is:

Respect for privacy, dignity and religious and cultural beliefs. The Charter standard is that all health services should make provision so that proper personal consideration is shown to you, for example by ensuring that privacy, dignity and religious and cultural beliefs are respected. Practical arrangements should include meals to suit all dietary requirements, and private rooms for confidential discussions with relatives.

It is recognised that for care practitioners to fulfill the requirement of this standard, they need to acquire knowledge about world religions and the cultural beliefs of their local communities. This book attempts to provide relevant information about different world religions, customs and beliefs and their implications on the individual's needs in a care setting.

SECTION I

RELIGIONS OF THE WORLD

BUDDHISM

Buddhism is based on the teachings of Gautama the Buddha, who was born about 563 BC in North India. He started his life as a young nobleman, who through his own efforts achieved Enlightenment, thus becoming known as Buddha. The word Buddha means someone who no longer experiences any hatred, craving or mental confusion, but has qualities such as wisdom, compassion and contentment.

The enlightenment which Buddha found was a middle way between extremes of luxury and self-torture. It was based on meditation and a simple life of self-control. His teaching is contained in the FOUR NOBLE TRUTHS.

These are as follows:

1.   Suffering is a part of life.

2.   Suffering is due to selfishness.

3.   Suffering will stop if selfishness is overcome.

4.   The way to bring suffering to an end is to follow the Eightfold Path.

The Enlightenment which Buddha achieved can be attained by following the Eightfold Path.

The Eightfold Path is:

1. Seeing the limitations of one's present life and experience, as well as the possibility of leading a more satisfying, fulfilling, truly human life.
2. Resolving to take the necessary steps to change oneself and one's life.
3. Practising truthful, kindly, harmonising speech; avoiding lies, backbiting and gossip.
4. Trying to avoid harming or exploiting other living beings (including animals, birds, fish, insects etc).
5. As far as possible earning one's living in a way which does not harm either oneself, others or the environment.
6. Avoiding harmful thoughts and actions and trying instead to develop good, kindly thoughts and feelings.
7. Learning to be aware of oneself, other people and one's surroundings.
8. Learning to concentrate one's mind through meditation.

TEMPLE / COMMUNITY CENTRE

Buddhist centre is a simple place of worship and meditation called a Vihara or a Meeting House. It will contain a shrine, and attached to the building may be accommodation with facilities for the community, and accommodation for a number of Buddhist teachers.

BUDDHIST TEACHERS / MONKS

The spiritual community is a very important part of Buddhism, which encourages and helps others to practice the teachings of Buddha. The more spiritually mature Buddhists are able to function as teachers and leaders. Some of these teachers become monks, and they play a vital role in the community. They are easy to recognise because they wear orange-coloured robes and have shaven heads. Sometimes they live, and to all appearances are, like other Buddhists.

SHRINE

Most Buddhists will make a shrine somewhere in their home. A typical shrine consists of a small table with a statue or image of Buddha in the centre with flowers, candles and sweet-smelling incense around it.

SPREAD OF BUDDHISM

Buddhism, as we have seen, began in Northern India and from there it spread to other parts of the sub-continent including Nepal, Tibet, Mongolia, Vietnam, Korea, Japan, Thailand, Kampuchea (Cambodia) and Sri Lanka. In recent years, there has been a steady increase in the number of Buddhists to be found in the west. It has been estimated that there are now over 130,000 practising Buddhists in Britain.

Statue of Buddha

DIET

Since Buddhism encourages its followers to practice non-violence, Buddhists will normally be vegetarians, or at least be taking steps in that direction. These meals vary considerably, depending upon their country of origin.

DRESS CODE

There is no special Buddhist dress. Men and women usually wear the dress of the country in which they live.

BIRTH & GROWING UP

As in most countries and religions, the birth of a child is a time of rejoicing. Parents may decide to give their child a Buddhist name and perhaps have a name-giving ceremony at the centre.

In a Buddhist family, children will be encouraged to respect their parents and to relate to them in a positive way. Buddhists place great emphasis on the health and education of their children and encourage them to look after their parents in old age.

MARRIAGE

Marriage in Buddhism is not a religious sacrament, but is simply a social arrangement.

FAMILY PLANNING

Buddhists believe that life begins at conception and so do not condemn contraception. However abortion is seen as taking life, thus it is condemned.

DEATH

Buddhists believe in rebirth after death. They also believe that their actions, whether good or bad, will have consequences, not just in this life but possibly in future lives too.

At a Buddhist funeral, there will be a general remembrance of, and a rejoicing in, the good qualities of the deceased. Those present will try to develop warm and friendly feelings for the dead person in the belief that this will help in the after-death state, before he or she is reborn. Finally the dead person is cremated.

CHRISTIANITY

Christians believe that Jesus was the Christ and the son of God. He was born in Bethlehem in Southern Palestine almost 2,000 years ago. When he was about 30 years old, he was baptised and he began a new life of teaching and healing. He travelled through the towns and villages of Palestine with twelve men whom he had chosen to be his companions. This lasted for less than three years until he came into serious conflict with the Roman authorities in Jerusalem, the most important Jewish city.

Jesus was arrested, tried, condemned to death and then crucified, nailed to a cross until he died.

It is believed that within three days, he had risen from the dead. His companions discovered that his tomb was empty and then they reported meeting, talking and sharing meals with him.

A few weeks later, they watched Jesus being taken to heaven by God, promising to return at the end of the world.

HOLY BOOK

The Christian Bible contains the complete Jewish Bible, which is called the Old Testament. To this was added a collection of books written during the hundred or so years after Jesus, which is known as the New Testament.

Anglican Cathedral - Liverpool

CHURCH

Christians can worship anywhere but they have built Churches since the end of the third century. The more important places of worship are known as Cathedrals. The services in Cathedrals or Churches are led by specially trained and ordained priests.

THE CENTRE OF FAITH

The common focus for all Christians is their belief in Jesus Christ who was the son of God, who lived on earth as a human and suffered pain and death and then rose from the dead. They believe God sent Jesus to show the world how much he loved it and to save the world from sin.

CHRISTIAN GROUPS

There are many different Christian groups and there are often great differences between one group and another. Such differences have led to a long tradition of debate, disagreement and disputes within the Christian family which has helped to shape a lively and vigorous faith. However the single concept of one God who reveals Himself as Father, Son and Holy Spirit is central to all Christian teaching.

Christian tradition recognises seven sacraments which are:

1. Baptism, the most important sacrament which marks the entry of a person into the faith.
2. The Eucharist, also known as the Holy Communion.
3. Confirmation.
4. Penance.
5. Matrimony.
6. Priestly Ordination.
7. Sacrament of the Sick.

Different churches vary in the importance they attach to the different sacraments.

The two most common Christian groups in the the UK are the Anglicans and the Roman Catholics. The third group known as The Free Churches is made up of several Christian groups which include the Methodists, Pentecostal and Quakers.

ANGLICANS or CHURCH OF ENGLAND

The Church of England's roots go back to the first Christians who came to Britain during the Roman times. King Henry VIII made the break with Rome and established the Church of England as the state church. About 57 percent of the population of the the UK is considered to be Anglicans.

ROMAN CATHOLICS

Roman Catholicism began with the followers of Jesus Christ. As well as their belief in Jesus Christ, they consider Mary, the mother of Christ to be the centre of their faith. Catholicism places greater emphasis on the sacraments and significance of worship than some other churches. About 13 percent of the population of the UK are followers of the Catholic faith.

Roman Catholics are expected to conform to a certain code which demands:

- They attend a church service every Sunday and certain other designated days in the year.

- Adults should fast on some days and abstain from eating meat on special religious days.

- Every Friday, they try to do without something and instead do something positive for someone else.

- They believe in confession, that is, they talk to a priest about sins which they believe they have committed and ask for God's forgiveness.

According to the Catholic faith, there are seven sacraments which every Catholic experiences as an outward sign of God's grace or favour.

BIRTH & GROWING UP

BAPTISM

Most Christians regard baptism as an outward, physical sign of re-birth. It marks the start of a new life which they share with other Christians and the water is a symbol of the way in which sin was removed from human life by Jesus.

The Roman Catholic, Orthodox and most Protestant Churches baptise children when they are still babies. During the service, the Minister makes the sign of the cross on the baby's forehead. The parents and godparents promise to help the baby grow up as a Christian.

CONFIRMATION

This ceremony is conducted whenever a Christian decides to "confirm" the promises made on his/her behalf at baptism.

MARRIAGE

Christians believe that marriage is central to human life because it marks the beginning of a new family and a new generation. The young people choose their own partners and have a say in whom they marry.

FAMILY PLANNING

Christian views on family planning vary considerably. Roman Catholics do not believe in any family planning devices, but in practice, individuals may vary in their approach. Anglicans do not have any objections.

SACRAMENT OF THE SICK

The Sacrament of the sick is a symbol of Christ's healing and loving. It can be adapted according to the severity of the illness and repeated if the circumstances change. If the person is dying, the priest anoints the dying person in a special ceremony which symbolises forgiveness, healing and reconciliation. For those who believe in these sacraments this service is of great significance.

DEATH

Christians are taught that Jesus will return to the world to rule forever and on this day, the dead will rise to join in His glory. In the past, most believed that they should be buried, not cremated. Generally speaking, Roman Catholics have continued this tradition and the Anglicans have moved more towards cremation.

CONFUCIANISM / TAOISM

CONFUCIANISM

Confucianism is the ancient religion of China. From about 400 BC (before Christ) to AD 1900, the teaching of the wise man Confucius was the main religion of the Chinese people.

In Chinese, Confucius' name - Kong Fu TZS means "The wise teacher Kong" and this is how, after more than 2,000 years, many Chinese people still think of him.

Confucius taught that if people followed his way, they would become good and holy and wise.

They would become what he called "NOBLE MINDED PEOPLE"

The five rules to follow are:
1.   GOODNESS
2.   JUSTICE
3.   RESPECT
4.   CONSIDERATION
5.   COURTESY

TAOISM

The great Taoist religion is in many ways the opposite of Confucianism. One major difference between the two religions was the Taoist quest for freedom. For some it was a freedom from the political and social constraints, for others it was a more profound search for immortality. Change itself was a very important part of the Taoist view of reality.

CROSS-FERTILIZATION

The great Chinese religions have always been influenced by each others development. The picture became even more complicated with the introduction of Buddhism into China. Both Taoism and Confucianism borrowed a great deal from Buddhism.

THE THREE ARE ONE

The great heyday of cross-fertilization of religions in China came in the 13th century. The best features of Taoist and Buddhist meditation were combined with the Confucian sense of shared concern for fellow creatures in a uniquely Chinese synthesis. This kind of religious life is still present in China today and in fact, it would not be far wrong to say that most religious Chinese draw on a mixture of all religions.

Chinese Pagoda

DIFFERENT CODES FOR DIFFERENT NEEDS

The Chinese have scores of Gods from whom they seek help at different times and for different reasons. The Gods are important as the Chinese believe that when they die, they will go before ten judges of the underworld who punish evil people.

Most Chinese Gods stem from either Taoism or Buddhism. Taoist Gods are either legendary figures or real people who have achieved fame during their lives.

PRACTICAL MATTERS

Chinese people have a very practical approach to their religion. They consult their Gods on such matters as career prospects, important dates, or during illness.

PRAYER/WORSHIP

Worship is a daily event for many Chinese and praying is a personal affair. There are no special holy days or priests to take services. Even when people pray together aloud, they seldom use the same prayer.

In 1949, the Chinese Communists proclaimed their country a Peoples Republic. Since then, religion has been discouraged and Communist ideas have dominated.

DIET

Chinese believe that in order to be healthy, an equilibrium between hot and cold needs to be maintained, be it in the form of food, herbs or medicines.

All Chinese foods are classified as hot or cold, so in order to restore balance, they must adhere to a special diet. Rice and noodles are the staple food of the Chinese, and are eaten with a variety of meat, fish and vegetable dishes. Chinese meals have greatly influenced eating habits in the western world.

DRESS CODE

Most Chinese wear western clothes. Older females tend to wear trousers and tunic.

IDEAS OF MODESTY

In general, Chinese women are very shy and modest. They prefer to be examined by a female doctor.

BIRTH & GROWING UP

Traditionally large families are a source of pride. The birth of a son is still celebrated, as boys represent security and are expected to look after their ageing parents. Families are very close knit and children are taught to respect their parents from an early age. Children also learn to respect their ancestors. Ancestor worship is the way a family honours an ancestor's achievements in life.

MARRIAGE

Arranged marriages used to be the traditional method of getting married. Fortune tellers are consulted, using the couple's birthdays, but the parents have the final decision. Matchmaking is rare these days as most young people choose whom they wish to marry, although they still prefer to get their parents' consent.

FAMILY PLANNING

Chinese accept family planning devices and even abortions. They now put more emphasis on the quality of the upbringing of their children rather than the size of the family. The idea of having a balance of male and female children is growing, though the preference for male descendants is still strong amongst more traditionally-minded parents.

Family Planning matters should not be mentioned in the presence of other Chinese.

DEATH

Funeral and mourning customs vary widely amongst the Chinese, depending upon their beliefs. Some Chinese are buried, whilst others are cremated. Traditionally, a dead person gets the best funeral a family can afford. Relatives grieve dressed in white or beige gowns. Chinese express grief openly and in public.

HINDUISM

Hinduism is not just a single religion but a collection of different forms of Indian beliefs. It is the third largest religion after Christianity and Islam. Estimates of the size of the Hindu community in the UK vary considerably. A widely accepted estimate is about 400,000 people.

Hinduism began about 2,000 years before the life of Jesus Christ and did not have a founder like most other religions. Hindus believe that BRAHMAN is the supreme spirit of all creation. It is perfect and unchanging and is neither male nor female. Brahman created the Hindu gods. There are hundreds of these, but the three most important ones are:

1.   BRAHMA - The Creator of Life
2.   VISHNU - The Preserver of Life
3.   SIVA - The Destroyer of Life

All these gods and goddesses are seen as the many manifestations of the same God.

Hindus believe that the soul must be cleansed of earthly sins before it can return to Brahman (The Creator).

KARMA (Actions) & REBIRTH

Hindus believe that a person's Karma is formed by his or her good and bad deeds, and by the religious merits gained in each life. Karma is formed as the cause and effect of all that happens in one's life. This Karma controls what a person will be in his or her next life. In Hindu belief, the human soul does not necessarily have to be reborn in a human body. A person with a very bad Karma may be reborn as an animal or even as an insect. The wheel of life continues turning until the soul is pure enough to return to the Spirit of Creation.

SALVATION THROUGH YOGA

Good deeds alone are not enough to purify the soul. Certain religious duties and rituals may also help. One action that helps to develop good Karma is Yoga. Yoga means "union". In this case, it means union of the human mind with Brahman. Yoga is a form of deep meditation that is aided by certain positions and controls of the body, as well as control of the mind.

VEDAS

These are religious books of knowledge, the oldest of which is the RIG-VEDA. It was written in 1,000 BC, but existed in oral form before this date.

SHRI BHAGVAT GITA

This is the most commonly used Holy Book out of which verses are recited at various religious ceremonies.

HINDU WAY OF LIFE

To be a Hindu, there are certain things that one must believe in and live by. These are:

1. A belief in KARMA - the result of one's good and bad deeds in life.

2. A belief in DHARMA - the traditions of Hinduism and inherent individual qualities.

3. A belief in GODS - BRAHMA, VISHNU & SIVA.

4. A belief that the soul is reborn after death in a new body.

5. Reverence for the Sacred Vedas.

6. A belief that the Soul can by means of a religious life, liberate itself from the wheel of life.

7. Reverence for an Ascetic religious life.

8. "OM" is the symbol and sound of God.

TEMPLES & WORSHIP

Most Hindus today are followers of one of the personal gods. The centres of worship are the Temples, but some worship is also practised in the home. At certain times of the day, the head of the family will make offerings and say prayers before the image of the chosen god.

Hindu Temple - India

RIVER GANGES - HOLY RIVER

The river Ganges is regarded as a sacred river which has purifying and healing properties. Millions of Hindus visit the temples along the banks of the Ganges and bathe in its water. It is the wish of most Hindus that after their death, they have their ashes scattered on the river Ganges.

DRESS CODE

The female national costume of the country is a saree which is worn over a short blouse and an underskirt. The midriff is usually left bare.

BINDI - coloured red spot on forehead may be worn by married women.

The male costume of the sub-continent is a long jacket with high collar and buttons down the front, worn over western-style trousers. Most men wear western style clothes.

Woman in Saree

30

DIET

Hindus place great significance on a spiritual diet. They have a great love for animals because of their belief in reincarnation. For this reason, they do not believe in killing animals. Hindus believe a cow is the most sacred animal. Therefore, the killing of a cow is one of the greatest religious crimes. Hindus are very strict vegetarians. They will not accept food which has come in contact with prohibited foods.

THE STAGES OF HINDU LIFE

Hinduism is taught from the cradle and is ingrained in its followers. In addition, Hindu customs and culture are deeply rooted in the religion. Hinduism provides each person with a road map to follow through their entire life.

BIRTH & GROWING UP

When a baby is born in a Hindu family, there is great rejoicing and the priest is informed of the date and exact time of the child's birth. From this information, the baby's horoscope is prepared. Hindus accord great significance to astrology at such important stages of their lives. The priest will then suggest suitable syllables from which the parents select a name for the baby. This is one of the main reasons why Hindus do not register the name of their baby immediately in western countries.

HAIR CUTTING CEREMONY

Many boys go through a ceremony when they have their first haircut. Their head is completely shaved. The symbolic meaning of this ceremony is that bad impressions from the previous life are removed.

UPANAYANA

This is one of the important ceremonies when a Hindu boy is given a thread with three strands which he wears on his body. This thread is a symbol of his second birth when he starts to learn from his Guru (Teacher). The three strands symbolise his duties to God, his parents and teachers and to the world.

MARRIAGE

Most Hindu marriages are arranged by the parents and the marriage is seen as a unity of two souls through two families rather than two individuals. The marriage day and time is fixed by the priest after reference to astrology.

FAMILY PLANNING

There is no Hindu objection to family planning from the religious point of view. However, there may be strong social and family pressures on the woman, particularly if no son has yet been born. It is advisable for the husband to be involved in any discussion of family planning.

DEATH

The dying person is read passages from the Holy Book and prayers are said. Thread similar to that worn by young boys with three strands may be tied around the wrist. The forehead is marked with a holy paste. It is believed that after death, the soul immediately leaves the body to start its new life and as it is the hope of every Hindu not to be reborn but to achieve unity with God. God's name is repeated into the ears of the dying person.

Hindus believe that a body without a soul is a carcass which must return to nature, thus they are cremated. Because of the strong belief in this, a dying person may occasionally request to be placed on the ground during the final few breaths. The ashes of the dead are scattered either in the sea or river, preferably in the river Ganges. Children under the age of five are buried.

Hindus prefer to cremate the body as soon as possible after death before the next sunset. If the body is to be left in a room overnight, a light or a candle must be left burning throughout the night.

ISLAM

The word **Islam** means submission and the followers of the religion are known as Muslims. Islam is a world wide religion founded by Prophet Mohammed in Saudi Arabia in the sixth century AD. Muslims believe in one God - ALLAH.

The religious duty of the Muslims is summed up in *Five Pillars* as follows:

1. CREED - God is one and only one supreme Creator, and Mohammed is the prophet of God.

2. PRAYER - Prayer is an essential part of religion and Muslims are required to pray according to set rituals, five times a day.

3. ALMSGIVING - Each person is asked to contribute a proportion of their income to the poor.

4. FASTING - This takes place for a whole month - the month of RAMADAN. The Islamic year consists of 354 days (11 days shorter than the International year), therefore the month of Ramadan occurs during all four seasons of the

year in 33 year cycles. During this month, all Muslims must fast from dawn to sunset. The sick, the aged, children and nursing mothers are excused from fasting.

5. PILGRIMAGE - Once in a lifetime, if possible, every Muslim is expected to make a pilgrimage to Mecca, the Muslim's Holy City.

Dome of the Rock

THE MOSQUE & WORSHIP

The mosque is the religious centre which plays an important part in the lives of Muslim men. Men and women are segregated into different rooms. The Islamic religion dictates that all Muslims pray five times a day. The prayer itself has a set of rituals which are carried out whilst kneeling on a special mat and facing towards Mecca, their Holy City.

THE KORAN (QURAN)

This is the most sacred scripture of Islam. Muslims believe that the scripture in Koran are Allah's (God's) commands which were revealed to Prophet Mohammed.

PRIESTHOOD

There is no priesthood in Islam and no titles for religious officials. Anyone who knows the Koran and the Islamic way of life can lead the prayer. The one who leads the prayer is called IMAM (leader).

THE SPREAD OF ISLAM

There are Muslims in almost every country in the world. In more than fifty countries, Islam is the biggest religion. Most Muslims live in the great belt stretching from Morocco to Pakistan.

Indonesia, followed by Bangladesh and Pakistan have the largest population but there are also tens of millions of Muslims living as minority groups in India, China and Europe.

Islamic Woman (Algerian)

36

MUSLIMS IN BRITAIN

Britain's Muslim population is very mixed, ranging from students from Nigeria and Malaysia, businessmen from the Middle East and East Africa and former farmers from Pakistan, Bangladesh and India. The estimated population of Muslims in the UK is about 1,500,000.

DIET

Diet has spiritual significance. Muslims are forbidden to eat pork or pork products. In addition, a Muslim cannot consume the meat of animals or birds which is not ritually slaughtered. Meat which satisfies the Muslim religious laws is known as HALAL. This is the same principle as *KOSHER* food for Jews. Alcohol is forbidden, but not tobacco.

DRESS CODE

The Islamic religion has high moral values which demand:

- men and women are separated in public places.
- women keep their bodies covered, apart from their faces, at all times, especially in public places.
- women wear a head scarf and men wear a brimless hat.

BIRTH & CHILDHOOD

When Muslims become parents, they have a special responsibility to ensure that their children grow up understanding the faith. The very first thing a Muslim baby hears on coming into the world is the *SHAHADAH* (the profession of faith). The birth of a child, especially a boy, is a time of rejoicing.

NAMING A CHILD

Naming a child has a religious significance, therefore, names cannot be chosen before the birth of a baby.

Muslim boys are circumcised, usually while they are only few days old. This occasion is celebrated as a great religious event.

Muslim babies also have all their hair shaved as part of a religious ritual.

Most young children are sent to religious schools where they are taught to read the KORAN.

TEENAGERS

As teenagers, Muslims are expected to work hard at school and help around the house, especially the girls. Going out alone to parties, discos or clubs is discouraged, especially for girls. On the whole, girls tend to be treated more strictly than boys. Teenagers of both sexes, however, are expected to show great respect towards their older relatives and enjoy the company of their family.

MARRIAGES

In Islam, a happy family is regarded as the foundation of a healthy society. The Koran encourages Muslims to marry and have children. It also emphasises that sexual relationships outside marriage are always wrong. Marriages between Muslims are often arranged by the parents and marrying within the family, for example first cousins is encouraged. Muslim men are allowed to have up to four wives, but it is very rare for most ordinary men to have more than one wife. Muslims do, however, think that it is good to be able to have a second wife if the first is unable to have children. In such cases both wives live together as part of the family. In Britain due to the legal requirements the man has to officially divorce his first wife for the second marriage to take place.

EXTENDED FAMILY

In most Muslim countries, the family is a large group, consisting of grandparents, parents, many uncles, aunts and cousins, either in one household or very close to each other. Members of the large extended family network are expected to help each other. This concept of extended family support is difficult to maintain in the UK for many reasons. One main reason is the style of housing which restricts the number of people who can live together.

FAMILY PLANNING

Strictly speaking, orthodox Muslims do not approve of family planning devices. In practice, individuals vary widely in their approach.

DEATH

Muslims believe in the resurrection of the body after death, therefore they bury their dead. Burial is expected to take place as quickly as possible after death. The traditional reason for this is the effect of heat on the corpse. Before burial, the body is washed and wrapped in a shroud. A funeral prayer follows. It is a duty laid upon all Muslims to see that the believers of the faith have a proper funeral. Women do not usually attend the burial but often visit the grave for years afterwards.

JUDAISM

Judaism has been in existence for over five thousand years. Throughout its long history, the Jewish religion has had many leaders and prophets, but there is no single founder of the religion. Moses is recognised as the most important leader of the Jews.

The Jewish belief about God is simple. They believe there is only one God and he alone should be prayed to. He is the creator of the Universe. Judaism teaches that because God is good, so people should be good. The Jewish religion demands that Jews should love both God and all people. An important Jewish teaching is that as God chose them by giving them his laws, they see themselves as the *light to the nations*, which means teaching the world about their hopes of a united human race and peace.

THE BIBLE

The oldest sacred book of the Jewish people is the Bible. Christians refer to it as the OLD TESTAMENT, but Jews usually call it the TENACH. The first five books are considered the most important and in Hebrew they are called the TORAH. The contents of these books form the Torah

Scrolls, parts of which are read in the Synagogue each Monday, Thursday, Saturday (Sabbath) and on special Festive days.

RABBI

A religious leader of the Jewish faith is called a Rabbi.

The Wailing Wall - Jerusalem

THE SYNAGOGUE

The synagogue is the Jews' house of worship and is also used as a community centre. There are three daily prayer sessions - morning, afternoon and evening. Whenever possible, Jews' prayers should be said at a public service, but if this is not possible then prayers can be said at home or elsewhere.

ORTHODOX & PROGRESSIVE JEWS

Most of the world's Jews can be divided into two groups:
- Orthodox
- Non-orthodox or progressive

Orthodox Jews believe that the Torah is the word of God, given directly by God and written down by Moses. It is perfect and the laws it contains are eternal. They must be obeyed without question.

Non-orthodox Jews believe that while the Torah is certainly the word of God, it is also a human document. Parts of it speak to every generation and parts are not necessarily relevant in today's world. They believe that some laws are eternal, but others can be abolished or changed, and new customs can be introduced to help Jews cope with problems of the modern world.

43

SPREAD OF JUDAISM

Jews have been great travellers throughout history. Over the centuries, they have made contact with most parts of the world and the various groups of Jews today owe their differences to these early settlements. A small number of Jewish immigrants settled in Britain early this century, but it was in the 1930's that most arrived from Germany and the East European countries. The Jewish population of the UK is estimated at 300,000.

DRESS CODE

There is no special dress code, but it is a requirement that married women cover their heads when praying. Although there is no Jewish law demanding that men should cover their heads while they pray, it is a binding custom that they do. Any suitable headgear is acceptable, but many wear the KIPAH (skullcap).

DIET

Judaism promotes compassion for animals and according to their religious laws animals are slaughtered in a humane way. The meat from this slaughtering process is called KOSHER meat.

Most Jews will only eat Kosher meat and the very orthodox Jews will not eat Kosher meat which has been cooked in utensils used for cooking non-Kosher meat. To be on the safe side, some may eat only vegetarian meals.

Jews only eat meat of those animals which chew the cud and are cloven footed, such as sheep and cows. Pigs and rabbits are forbidden. Fish must have both fins and scales, such as salmon and trout; others are not eaten, and shellfish is forbidden. A further ruling states that meat and milk products cannot be eaten together. This means that they do not have milk in their drinks or cream with their deserts after a meat meal, and do not use butter on meat sandwiches.

FASTING

There are several minor fasts in the religious calendar but the prominent fast which almost every Jew observes is the YOM-KIPPUR, the day of atonement. This is a 25 hour fast, which usually falls in late September or early October. This day is considered to be the holiest day of the Jewish calendar, and one that is considered to set the path for the year to follow. If health permits, most Jews prefer to keep this day as a special day for fast and prayer.

BIRTH & GROWING UP

Jewish children are given both a common name and a Hebrew name at birth, usually that of a deceased ancestor in order to perpetuate the name. The Hebrew name has a

Jewish historical meaning. The common name may be chosen from among those that are popular at the time.

A boy is given his name during a circumcision ceremony which is a very important and ancient ritual. It is important that this ceremony takes place on the eighth day after birth except in exceptional circumstances due to ill-health. The ceremony is performed by a MOHEL, who is not necessarily a doctor or a Rabbi, but a specially trained religious Jew.

Most Jewish children attend two schools - their ordinary daytime school and a religious school on Sunday morning and some week-day evenings. Part of being Jewish is learning about the religion, so that it is properly understood. Boys must be able to read Hebrew by the time they are thirteen years old, an age which marks a boy's entry into manhood when he is expected to observe all the Jewish Laws.

MARRIAGE

Judaism encourages Jews to marry within the Jewish community. Although weddings do not have to be performed in Synagogues, most of them are. It is hoped that every marriage will result in the birth of children, for they are considered a very important link between the generations.

FAMILY PLANNING

While mechanical methods of contraception are not strictly permitted, today almost all Jews will use some method of family planning. According to Jewish law only women, not men, may use contraceptives for health reasons. Jewish law forbids contraception by men. The Pill is widely used by women.

DEATH

Jewish tradition demands that funerals and burials must take place as soon as possible after death, ideally within twenty four hours and usually within three days. The body is washed and shrouded by volunteer members of the Jewish faith before being placed in the coffin. Funeral services are always simple and the use of flowers is not encouraged. Cremation is not allowed among orthodox Jews, but it is common in the progressive groups.

SIKHISM

Sikhism is one of the youngest of the world's major religions. The Sikhs are people who follow the teachings of ten leaders who they call GURUS. All the Gurus lived between 1469 and 1708 in the part of northern India called Punjab.

The first Guru, known as Guru Nanak, was born in 1469. The main religions in India at that time were Hinduism and Islam. Members of these two religions followed practices which Guru Nanak rejected, such as rituals of idol worship, caste system, purdah (veiling) and sati (widow burning).

Sikhism is as much a way of life as a religion. Sikhs believe in ONE GOD. They are supposed to be distinguished by the five symbols, often referred to as the five K's, because of their Punjabi names which begin with that letter. The five K's are:

> Kesh - Uncut hair
> Kangha - Small comb used to keep the hair tidy
> Kara - Steel bangle
> Kaccha - Special shorts worn as underwear
> Kirpan - Dagger / Sword

Sikh men wear a turban to keep their hair in place. It is an insult to try and remove a person's turban.

GURU-GRANTH SAHIB

This is a holy book containing scriptures which is used at all religious services.

The Golden Temple - India

PRIESTHOOD

Although there are some specially trained priests, anyone can conduct the worship, provided the person is competent. Both men and women can act as priests.

SIKHISM - A WAY OF LIFE

The main ideals that influence the way of life for Sikhs are based on the following ideas:

1. EQUALITY

All human beings are equal because God is contained in every heart. The distinctions of cast, colour and creed only serve to perpetuate the inequalities which are created by selfish human beings. The Sikh concept of equality embraces both men and women in secular and religious life.

2. WORSHIP OF GOD

Sikhs believe God to be present everywhere, therefore prayer can be said anywhere at any time. The best times for prayers are considered to be before dawn and dusk.

3. DIGNITY OF LABOUR

Sikhism condemns idleness or a tendency to live off the work of others. For Sikhs there is a dignity in labour in any job, provided it is legal and ethical. Dishonesty is regarded as a serious sin.

4. GIVING TO CHARITY

The idea of living and sharing together is shown in the Sikh concern for the needs of the poor.

5. VOLUNTARY SERVICE

This plays an important part in the Sikh way of life.

THE SIKH CODE OF CONDUCT

- Sikhs are forbidden to cut their hair.
- Sikhs are forbidden to commit adultery.
- They are forbidden to smoke or chew tobacco.
- They are forbidden to eat Halal or Kosher meat.

SIKHS IN BRITAIN

Approximately 400,000 Sikhs live in Britain and they form the largest Sikh community outside India.

DIET

Many Sikhs do not eat beef because of the Hindu influence. While most will accept other meats, some women will not eat any kind of meat and may choose to be vegetarians. It is helpful to explain to individuals, whether dishes contain beef, pork or lamb, as they may not be familiar with names such as *Irish Stew or Scotch Broth*. Vegetarians will also find foods unacceptable if it has come in contact with meat dishes, for example serving food with the same serving spoon or cutting a cheese sandwich with the same knife which has been used for cutting meat sandwiches.

Tobacco and alcohol are discouraged.

DRESS CODE

Sikhs do not cut their hair and take great pride in keeping their hair clean and tidy. Most men wear a turban which clearly identifies their religion, but some do not because of social difficulties. In their own home they may choose not to wear a turban at all or use a substitute with a smaller head cover. Young Sikh boys may have their hair either plaited or tied in a knot which is then covered with a small handkerchief until such time as they are able to wear a turban.

Sikh Man

Men wear western clothes outside their home but may wear pyjamas with a long shirt at home or in hospital.

Women dress modestly, and wear a range of different clothing. Traditionally, they wear loose trousers and a long tunic with a long scarf called **CHUNI**. The scarf is used to cover their head as a mark of respect, especially when entering a place of worship. Young girls are encouraged to keep their legs covered when they reach their teens. Some older women will keep their head covered with a scarf at all times.

Sikh Woman

BIRTH AND GROWING UP

The birth of a baby is a time of rejoicing, especially if it is a boy. Sometimes the birth of a daughter appears to be a disappointment to the parents due to their desire for a son. Sons are seen as security, especially as the boys are expected to look after their ageing parents. This tradition has greater significance in countries where there are no social welfare systems to provide for the older population.

NAMING A CHILD

Soon after the birth of a child, the parents visit the temple to pray and decide on a name. This is done by opening the Holy Book at random, and the first letter of the first word on the left page is accepted as the letter with which the child's name must begin. For this reason, parents are unable to choose the name of their child before birth.

The first name is common to both sexes, and the second name is usually Singh for a boy and Kaur for a girl, followed by a family name (surname).

MARRIAGE

Marriage is particularly important for Sikhs as it is the basis for bringing up children in the Sikh faith. Marriage involves not just the couple, but also their families and because of this, the choice of a marriage partner is made with the advice and assistance of the families. Sikhs regard marriage as a sacred bond of mutual dependence between a man and a woman.

FAMILY PLANNING

Sikhs have no objection to family planning.

FAMILY LIFE

Sikh families, like most Indian families, have a tradition of extended or joint families. Sikhs maintain a strong and supportive family structure. Going to night clubs is discouraged especially for girls. All family members are encouraged to attend religious service, at the temple, especially on a Sunday.

DEATH

Sikhs believe in reincarnation, therefore death is seen as another stage of the life cycle. Following death, the room in which the body is laid must have a light switched on until it is removed. Traditionally, the funeral takes place before the next sunset. At Sikh funerals, families say goodbye to their dead relatives. The prayer said before going to bed is also recited at a funeral service, symbolising that death is similar to sleep and should not be mourned. The body is cremated and the ashes scattered in running water, for example in a river or sea.

SECTION II

WAY OF LIFE

ARABS

The majority of Arabs have emigrated from Saudi Arabia.

RELIGION

The religion followed by the community is Islam.

LANGUAGE

Arabic is the spoken language.

DRESS CODE

Arab Elder

Traditionally Saudi men wear a long white robe over western clothes which covers the entire body from neck to feet, with sleeves coming down to the wrists. They also cover the head with a headdress, which is usually made of white, or red and white chequered materials. The headdress is held in place by a double black cord called the egal.

Most Saudi women wear black in contrast to the men. Older women are generally dressed from head to toe in black. Younger women however may wear modern western clothes at home, but cover themselves with a silky black cloak called the Abbaya, and a scarf to cover their head when they go out in public.

Young Arab Woman

DIET

Arabs follow their Islamic religion on the subject of diet. They only eat Halal meat (animal slaughtered according to their religious method). They do not eat pork or pork products.

Traditional Arabic meals are meats or fish cooked with herbs and spices and served on a bed of rice. Plenty of fresh salad and special flat, circular bread are also very common and eaten with nearly all meals. Dates are popular and also form part of the staple diet.

Coffee is made and served with great ritual and ceremony. The drink is strongly flavoured and served in small cups.

FASTING

All Arabs fast during the Ramadan period, although the sick can be excused.

IDEAS OF MODESTY

Arab women are very modest and do not expose any part of their body in public. They prefer to be examined by female doctors. Women also prefer to wear long examination gowns and nightdresses. They will usually want to keep their head covered by wearing a scarf in hospital.

DEATH

Arabs bury their dead and express grief openly and publicly. The relatives will usually make all the arrangements for preparing the body for burial and all other rituals.

BANGLADESHIS

People who originate from Bangladesh, formerly East
Pakistan, are Bangladeshi.

RELIGION

The religion followed by the majority of the population, is
Islam, but a small proportion may be Hindus.

LANGUAGE

Bengali is the spoken language.

DRESS CODE

Bangladeshi women wear a saree, one end of which can be
used as a veil to cover their head.

Most men wear western clothes outside, but some will wear
a long shirt over trousers or pyjamas. They also often wear
a white cloth cap.

DIET

Islamic Bangladeshis do not eat pork or pork products. They are allowed only Halal meat (animal slaughtered according to the Islamic religion). Bangladeshis following the Hindu faith will be vegetarians and most Bangladeshis will accept a vegetarian meal to play safe. They find western substitutes for a vegetarian meal unacceptable, for example cheese salad or baked beans on toast. Some may not be used to eating with a knife and fork. Most eastern populations use their fingers and spoons for eating.

Rice is the staple food which is eaten with meat, fish, eggs, vegetables and salads. The dishes are usually highly spiced.

FASTING

Most patients in hospital are excused from fasting during the month of Ramadan.

ABLUTION

Bangladeshis attach great importance to washing in free-flowing water, and therefore prefer a shower. They find sitting in a bath unacceptable. Washing hands in free-flowing water is essential before eating meals, saying prayers and after visiting the toilet.

Bangladeshi Bride & Groom

IDEAS OF MODESTY

Bangladeshi women are usually very modest. As their
religion encourages them to keep their bodies covered at all
times, they may find it embarrassing to wear a short, open
gown for special investigations. A blanket or long gown
could be helpful to cover their bodies. Due to cultural

upbringing, Muslim women prefer to see female doctors, especially when intimate procedures are about to be carried out. Single sex wards or a single room are greatly appreciated.

PRAYER

Prayer is an essential part of the Bangladeshi way of life and Muslims are required to pray according to a set of rituals five times a day. This requires privacy, therefore either a single room for the patient's use or a room especially set aside for prayers is required.

DEATH

Islamic Bangladeshis prefer to bury the body as soon as possible. Permission for a post-mortem is only given if legally required. Grief is openly expressed. The family will accept responsibility for making all the necessary arrangements. In Muslim countries, the mourning period varies from seven days to forty days and can even be up to three months. During this period, no joyful events such as weddings, take place.

CHINESE

The Chinese have very rich and varied religious traditions and an extremely complex system of magical beliefs. The younger generations have adapted well to the western influences, but there still remains a group of older Chinese who have held on to their cultural beliefs.

RELIGIONS

Taoism and Buddhism are the main religions although some Chinese are Christians.

LANGUAGE

There are several different dialects spoken by the Chinese. They are - Cantonese, Chiu-Chow, Hakki, Mandarin and See-Yip. Cantonese is the most commonly spoken.

DRESS CODE

Most Chinese wear western clothes. Older females tend to wear trousers and tunics.

Chinese Bride & Groom

DIET

The Chinese believe that in order to be healthy, an equilibrium between hot and cold needs to be maintained, be it in the form of food, herbs or medicines. Foods are classified as hot or cold. Therefore, in order to restore balance, the Chinese may adhere to a special diet. Rice is the staple food of the Chinese which is eaten with a variety of meat, fish and vegetable dishes. Chinese meals have greatly influenced western eating habits.

IDEAS OF MODESTY

In general, Chinese women are very shy and modest. They prefer to be examined by a female doctor, although medical care takes priority should female doctors not be available.

DEATH

Funeral and mourning customs vary widely amongst the Chinese, depending upon their beliefs. Some are buried, whilst others are cremated. Individual family wishes are repected. Relatives grieve dressed in white or beige clothes if they follow the traditional religions, but black if they are Christians.

INDIANS - GUJARATIS

The two main centres of emigration from India are the states of Gujarat and Punjab. The religion, culture and way of life of both groups are markedly different.

GUJARATIS

The Gujarati community comes from the state of Gujarat which is on the north west coast of India.

RELIGION

The religion followed by the community is mainly Hinduism, but a small proportion are Muslims.

LANGUAGE

Hindi is the administrative language of India, but Gujarati is the first spoken language.

DRESS CODE

Women wear a saree over a short blouse and underskirt. The midriff is usually left bare.

BINDI

A coloured spot on the forehead indicates whether a lady is married or not. A red spot means the lady is married. Different colours to match an outfit are used by young single girls. A black spot is worn by widows.

Most men wear western clothes. At home or in hospital, they may wear a long white shirt and pyjamas.

DIET

The diet varies considerably depending upon the person's religion. Hindus place great significance on spiritual diet. They believe that it is wrong to take life, therefore they are strict vegetarians. They will not accept food which has come into contact with prohibited food.

Rice is the staple food which is eaten with a combination of vegetables, salads and pickles.

Indians prefer to eat their traditional meals with their fingers or a spoon.

FASTING

Fasting is considered as a spiritual and physical benefit, and is a personal decision. Most patients in hospital do not fast.

ABLUTION

Gujaratis attach great importance to cleanliness and prefer a daily shower. A bath is considered unhygienic.

Gujarati Groom & Bride

IDEAS OF MODESTY

Women prefer to wear long gowns and nightdresses as they find exposing their legs embarrassing. Out of choice, women would prefer to be examined by a female doctor.

DEATH

Hindus believe in reincarnation and cremate their dead, as they believe that the soul leaves the body at death. Muslims believe in burial. They prefer to bury the body as soon as possible. Permission for a post-mortem is only given if legally required. Grief is openly expressed. The family will accept the responsibility of making all the necessary arrangements for cremation.

INDIANS - HINDUS

The Indian name for the sub-continent is "HINDUSTAN" meaning land of Hindus.

RELIGION

Hinduism is the main religion of India.

LANGUAGE

Hindi is the administrative language of the country, but Urdu is also understood by most.

DRESS CODE

The female national costume of the country is a saree which is worn over a short blouse and an underskirt. The midriff is usually left bare.

The male costume of the sub-continent is a long jacket with a high collar and buttons down the front, worn over western style trousers. However, most men wear western style clothes. In hospital, men will usually wear long shirts over pyjamas.

BINDI - This coloured red spot on the forehead may be worn by married women.

DIET

Hindus place great significance on a spiritual diet. They have a great love of animals because of their belief in reincarnation. For this reason, they do not believe in killing animals. Hindus believe the cow is the most sacred animal. Hence, the killing of a cow is one of the greatest religious crimes. Hindus are normally very strict vegetarians. They will not accept food which has come into contact with prohibited food. Rice and chapatti are both eaten with various vegetables, pulses, and yoghurt. Pickles and salads are commonly used as side dishes.

FASTING

Fasting is considered to give both spiritual and physical benefits, and is a personal choice. Sick and elderly people are not expected to fast.

ABLUTIONS

Like most Asians, Hindus attach great importance to personal cleanliness. They prefer showers to baths. Washing hands in free flowing water before meals and before prayers is essential.

Toilet paper on its own is not considered hygienic, therefore water must be available in the toilet. Washing hands after the using a bedpan is also considered essential.

Hindu Groom & Bride

IDEAS OF MODESTY

Hindu women prefer to wear long gowns and nightdresses as they find exposing their legs embarrassing. The older female population prefers to be examined by a female doctor. However, medical care takes priority over the availability of a female doctor in an emergency. Older women will not wear short open back gowns.

DEATH

Hindus believe in cremating the body, preferably before the next sunset, or if not, as soon as possible. If the body has to be left overnight, then a light must be left on in the room throughout the dark hours.

After the cremation ceremony, the ashes are collected and scattered over running water like a river. The wish of most Hindus will be to have their ashes scattered over the river Ganges - "The Holy River".

Relatives will fully participate in making all arrangements.

A child under five years of age is usually buried rather than cremated.

INDIANS - SIKHS

During the partition of India, the state of Punjab was split. More than half of Punjab became part of West Pakistan and the remainder stayed as part of India. The majority of Sikhs come from Punjab in India.

RELIGION

The religion practised by the majority of the community is Sikhism.

LANGUAGE

Punjabi is the most common first language, but Hindi or Urdu is understood by most.

DRESS CODE

Women wear a long tunic over loose trousers and a long scarf. Young girls are encouraged to keep their legs covered from an early age. Most men wear western clothes and a turban. Young boys have their hair either plaited or tied in a knot on top of their head, which is usually covered with a white hankie.

DIET

Sikhs observe fewer dietary restrictions than Hindus or Muslims. However some are very strict vegetarians and most will not eat beef.

ABLUTION

Like most Asians, Sikhs attach great importance to cleanliness. They prefer showers to baths. Washing hands in free-flowing water before meals, prayers and after visiting a toilet is considered essential.

Sikh Bride & Groom

IDEAS OF MODESTY

Older females prefer to be examined by female doctors, but medical care takes priority over the availability of male/female doctors. Older women will not wear short open back gowns. Men will usually wear a long shirt with pyjamas and will keep their turban on except when going to bed.

DEATH

Death is accepted as part of the cycle of reincarnation. Sikhs prefer to cremate the body as soon as possible, preferably before the next sunset. If the body has to be left in a room overnight, a light must be left on throughout. Ashes are scattered in running water. Relatives will accept the responsibility of making all the necessary arrangements. A child under the age of five is usually buried rather than cremated.

PAKISTANIS

People who originate from Pakistan are known as Pakistanis.

RELIGION

The religion followed by the population is Islam.

LANGUAGE

Urdu is the administrative language of Pakistan. Pakistanis can usually speak Punjabi, Urdu or Hindi.

DRESS CODE

Pakistani women dress very modestly, covering their body completely with the exception of their face. They usually wear a long tunic over loose trousers and a long scarf. When in the presence of mixed company, they may cover their head with a scarf.

Men usually wear western clothes outside the home, and pyjamas with a long shirt at home or in hospital.

DIET

Pakistanis do not eat pork or pork products. They prefer Halal meat (animals slaughtered according to Islamic religion). Most will accept a vegetarian meal to play safe. Chapatti, which is made out of wheat, is the staple food. Rice is not uncommon. These staples are eaten with highly spiced meat, fish and vegetable dishes. Salads are eaten with a meal as a side dish. Pakistanis find western substitutes for a vegetarian meal unacceptable, for example cheese salad or baked beans on toast. Some may not be used to eating with a knife and fork. Most eastern populations use their fingers and spoons for eating.

FASTING

Most patients in hospital are excused from fasting during Ramadan.

ABLUTION

Pakistanis attach great importance to washing in free-flowing water, therefore prefer a shower. They find sitting in a bath unacceptable. Washing hands in free-flowing water before eating meals, saying prayers and after visiting the toilet is considered essential.

Pakistani Groom & Bride

IDEAS OF MODESTY

Pakistani women are generally very modest. As their religion encourages them to keep their bodies covered at all times, they may find it embarrassing to wear a short, open gown for special medical investigations. A blanket or long gown could be helpful to cover their bodies. Many women also prefer to keep their head covered with a scarf. Due to their cultural upbringing, Muslim women prefer to see female doctors, especially when intimate procedures are to be carried out. Single sex wards or a single room are greatly appreciated.

PRAYER

Prayer is an essential part of Pakistani life and Muslims are required to pray according to a set of rituals five times a day. This requires privacy, therefore, either a single room for the patient's use or a room especially set aside for prayers is required.

DEATH

Muslims prefer to bury the body as soon as possible. Permission for a post-mortem is only given if legally required. Grief is openly expressed. The family will accept responsibility for making all the necessary arrangements. In Muslim countries, mourning periods vary from seven days to forty days, and can even be up to three months. During this period, no joyful events take place, such as weddings.

RASTAFARIANS

The Rastafarian movement was started in Jamaica in the 1930s by Marcus Garvey, a black leader who said that an African King would save and help black people.

The original name of Ethiopia's Emperor Haile Selassie I was Ras Tafari. The Rastafarian faith is named after him. Rastafarians believe in one true God - Haile Selassie and that they will all return to Africa, their true home and that they will be free.

RASTAFARIAN WAY OF LIFE

Rastafari is a way of life and not a religion. They have many links with the Christian and Jewish faiths. Rastafarians are taught never to cut their hair, as it is a symbol of strength. The long braids are called dreadlocks which represent the lion's mane and the hair of an African warrior.

LANGUAGE

The language used by the Rastafarians is based on a Jamaican patois. Sentences are constructed with little use of verbs, and consequently others non-Rastafarians may not understand the speech.

Rastafarian Family

DRESS CODE

Rastafarians usually wear ordinary western clothes. On holy days, white clothes are often worn which are made in an African style. Certain colours such as green, red, gold and black have a specific significance. A traditional Rastafarian hat, called a tam, is worn by some men and women to keep their hair covered.

DIET

Most Rastafarians do not eat meat or salt. Many do not eat fish, eggs or dairy products. Some do not consume milk or coffee and prefer fresh vegetables and fruit. They believe that a healthy diet is an important part of a healthy lifestyle.

FAMILY PLANNING

The majority of Rastafarians do not believe in family planning.

COMMUNITY HALL

Rastafarians do not always have special buildings, so they conduct their religious meetings weekly in a local Community Hall. There is always music which accompanies the hymns and songs. Rastafarian music is called reggae. Through reggae, they sing about their beliefs and their lives.

CHAPLAIN

Meetings are led by the Chaplain who has a special duty to visit the sick and infirm.

DEATH

Rastafarians believe in the resurrection of the soul after death, but not of the flesh. Generally speaking, burial is the preferred choice but some may choose to be cremated. The funeral service is very simple and is usually attended by family and friends only.

SOMALIS

People who come from Somalia (the horn of Africa) are called Somalis. They have a dark colour, slim features and are generally taller than other Africans.

RELIGION

The religion practised by the Somalis is Islam. They are expected to pray five times a day.

LANGUAGE

The language spoken by the people is Somali, which had no written form until 1972. For this reason older Somali people are unable to read or write. The English alphabet is used for the written form.

DRESS CODE

Somali women wear long gowns which cover them from neck to ankles called the JUBA. They also wear a scarf to keep their head covered. Men usually wear western traditional clothes and will sometimes wear a white cloth cap as well.

DIET

Somalis do not eat pork or pork products. They will eat Halal meat only, which is animal slaughtered according to their religious belief. Alcohol is strictly prohibited.

Men tend to chew QAT which is part of a plant grown in Africa. Its effects on the individual may be similar to alcohol, such as hangovers and headaches. It is addictive and the desire to chew can lead to restlessness.

FASTING

During the religious month of Ramadan, Somalis will fast from sunrise to sunset. However, young, elderly and sick people can be excused if necessary.

ABLUTION

Somalis attach great importance to cleanliness. They prefer showers to baths because of their belief in washing in free-flowing water. They require water for washing in toilets, as paper on its own is not considered adequate. They wash their hands before they say their prayers.

PRAYER

Prayer is a very important part of the way of life. Somalis are required to pray five times a day, so will require a quiet room for this purpose. If possible a single room should be provided to meet their religious needs, especially if the wards cater for both sexes.

Somali Groom & Bride

IDEAS OF MODESTY

Islamic religion teaches high moral values which include:

- the separation of men and women in public places.
- women to keep their bodies covered, apart from their face at all times.

Somali women will not wear short open gowns, therefore, long gowns should be made available. They may also refuse to be examined by male doctors.

DEATH

Somalis prefer to bury their dead as soon as possible. Permission for a post-mortem is only given if legally required. Grief is openly expressed. The family will accept responsibility for making all the necessary arrangements. The mourning periods vary from seven days to forty days and can even be up to three months. During this period, no joyful events take place, such as weddings.

VIETNAMESE

Half the population of Vietnam is of Chinese origin. Therefore their customs and beliefs are very similar to those of the Chinese.

RELIGION

Vietnam has no official religion and the population are followers of Confucianism, Taoism, Buddhism or a combination of these. The Communist Government now officially discourages religious worship.

LANGUAGE

Vietnamese is the official language, but there are two different dialects which may be spoken, depending on whether the individual comes from North or South Vietnam.

DRESS CODE

Most Vietnamese wear western clothes.

DIET

Like the Chinese, the Vietnamese hold the belief that in order to be healthy, an equilibrium between hot and cold needs to be maintained. Their meals are rice-based with plenty of vegetables and fish dishes. Meals can vary according to different religious beliefs.

Older Vietnamese people may not be used to eating with knives and forks, therefore, alternatives will need to be considered.

Vietnamese Groom & Bride

IDEAS OF MODESTY

In general, Vietnamese women are very shy and modest. They prefer to be examined by a female doctor if possible, but medical care takes priority over the availability of male/female doctors.

Women may find wearing short, open-back gowns unacceptable.

DEATH

Funeral and mourning customs vary widely according to religion and belief. Individual family wishes must be respected.

SECTION III

OTHER USEFUL INFORMATION

BRIEF HISTORY
of Bangladesh, India and Pakistan

In order to understand the cultures, beliefs and religions of these three countries, it is essential to have some knowledge of their history and the outside influences upon them.

The three countries as we know them today, have emerged from one country which was known as India. The religion followed by the people of this country was Hinduism.

- Outside influences from the middle east introduced the Islamic religion into the north-west of the country.

- Europeans discovered India, which was colonised by the British. This introduced Christianity into southern parts of the country.

- Due to the conflicting views amongst Hindus and Muslims in the north-west of India, a new religion emerged in the state of Punjab which is known as Sikhism.

Thus it can be seen that this vast country has had numerous political/religious influences upon its cultural beliefs.

Conflict between the Muslims and the Hindus continued. In 1947, India gained independence from the British and the country was partitioned into two countries which were then known as Pakistan and India.

Pakistan consisted of two areas with large Muslim populations, East Pakistan and West Pakistan, which were hundreds of miles apart.

Following a Civil War in 1971, East Pakistan became the Independent Republic of Bangladesh.

IMPROVING COMMUNICATION

Communication is a process through which a person receives, analyses and responds to messages. These messages can be warm and friendly or they can be cold and unfriendly. Two-way communication between the practitioner and the client/carer is of fundamental importance in health care. Communication with people who are not fluent in English can lead to some major difficulties and is often identified as a main reason for these individuals not accessing services.

NON-VERBAL COMMUNICATION

Non-verbal messages can create a friendly or hostile environment. Body language conveys very strong messages between individuals. If these messages are friendly, the person receiving them will respond in a positive way, but if they are unfriendly, the person will avoid or ignore them. Health workers need to be aware of other culture's body language.

Eye contact

According to western culture, direct eye contact is an important aspect of communication, whereas in eastern culture, it is considered a sign of defiance, thus not encouraged. This avoidance of eye contact is often mistaken as a sign that the person is lacking in confidence.

Touch

In the western culture touch is considered an acceptable form of communication, especially shaking hands. Some eastern women may find it unacceptable, especially with men. This is due to their very strict moral upbringing. Sikh men regard their turban as a religious symbol and prefer no one to touch it.

VERBAL COMMUNICATION

When communicating with people who are not fluent in English, the hints below can be helpful:
- make sure you pronounce unfamiliar names correctly
- speak clearly without raising your voice
- do not speak quickly
- keep sentences simple
- use clear logical order
- if you are not understood, repeat the same words again. If this fails, try to put your message in a completely different way. Speaking very loudly rarely makes a message better understood
- try not to use expressions only used in English such as *spend a penny*
- do not speak broken English
- focus on one thing at a time. Make sure your client understands before moving on
- using pictures may be helpful
- ask for an interpreter/link worker to assist.

INTERVIEWING WITH AN INTERPRETER

1. The interpreter should have time before the interview to talk with the client and the professional in order to establish some sort of relationship.

2. Interviews through an interpreter take longer than normal, possibly twice as long. Always allow sufficient time for this.

3. Remember that even when translating word for word, other languages are not always as concise as English. Do not get impatient if it feels as if the interpreter is taking too long with the client.

4. Do not tell the interpreter anything you do not want translated to the client.

5. For the purpose of confidentiality, any accompanying relatives or friends should not be present at the interview, unless requested by the client.

6. The seating arrangement should allow for direct eye contact amongst the three participants.

7. Welcome the client. Address him or her by name and confirm which name the client prefers to be addressed by.

8.   Encourage the interpreter and client to seek clarification if he/she does not understand something that has been said.

9.   Sometimes the interpreter may need to let the client talk on if the client is upset or emotional. Frequent interruptions may inhibit the client from revealing his/her feelings.

      Trust the interpreter's judgement and allow him/her to stop the client when he/she feels it is appropriate.

10.   Summarise what has been agreed. Ask if there is anything else he/she wants to know.

11.   Plan another interview if necessary and use the same interpreter if possible.

POINT TO REMEMBER WHEN USING INTERPRETERS

1. The interpreter is an equal member of the care team and is there to facilitate communication between the staff and the client.

2. Remember, the interpreter may have to develop a relationship of trust and co-operation with both sides.

3. Be aware of your own verbal and non-verbal messages, both towards the client and the interpreter.

4. The interpreter may need to act as an advocate for the client.

5. The interpreter should not be asked to take on duties other than interpreting and advocacy, such as giving advice.

6. The interpreter is not responsible for the client's behaviour or complaints, nor for the decisions of the professionals.

7. The interpreter's cultural knowledge is very important. As part of his/her duty, the interpreter can

advise professionals on cultural matters, enabling them to give better service to the client.

8.   Please make sure the interpreter's time is not wasted.

9.   Remind the interpreter of the need to respect confidentiality.

PRACTICAL THINGS TO DO

1.   Check that the interpreter and the client speak the same language or dialect.

2.   As far as possible, arrange for the interpreter to be of the same gender as the client.

3.   Allow time for pre-interview discussion with the client and the professionals.

4.   Allow sufficient time for the interview.

5.   Ensure a quiet area/room is available for the interview.

6.   Use simple language.

7.   Actively listen to the interpreter and involve the clients.

8.   Observe non-verbal messages between the group.

9.   Encourage open discussion.

10.   At the end of the interview check whether the client has understood everything and is aware of the plan.

11.   Have a post-interview meeting with the interpreter.

GREETINGS

ENGLISH
> **GOOD MORNING**
> **GOOD AFTERNOON**
> **GOOD EVENING**

ARABIC
> **SUBAH ELKHER**

صباح الخير

BENGALI
> **AVIVADAN SUPROVAT**

অভিবাদন
সুপ্রভাত

CHINESE
> **JO SUN**

早晨

HINDI
> **NAMESTE**

नमस्ते

PUNJABI
> **SAT SIRI AKAL**

ਸਤਿ ਸ੍ਰੀ ਅਕਾਲ

SOMALI
> **SALAAN**
> **SUBAX WANAAGSAN**

URDU
> **ALSALAM ALAIKUM**

السلام علیکم

WELCOME

ENGLISH
    WELCOME

ARABIC
    MARHABA

مرحبا

BENGALI
    SWAGWATAM
    SUVASAUN

স্বাগত সুভাষন

CHINESE
    FOON YING

歡迎

HINDI
    SWAAGTAM

स्वागतम्

PUNJABI
    JEE AAYAN NOON

ਜੀ ਆਇਆਂ ਨੂੰ

SOMALI
    SOO DHAWOW

URDU
    KHUSH AAMDEID

خوش آمدید

THANK YOU

ENGLISH
     THANK YOU

ARABIC
     SHOOKRAN

شكراً

BENGALI
     DHANNVAD

ধন্যবাদ

CHINESE
     DOOR TSE

多謝

HINDI
     DHANNYAVAD

धन्यावाद

PUNJABI
     DHANNVAD

ਪੰਨਵਾਦ

SOMALI
     MAHADSANID

URDU
     SHUKRYA

شُکریہ

ASIAN NAMING SYSTEMS

All Asian naming systems have a religious significance. In practice, they can vary considerably.

NAMING A BABY

Names cannot be chosen until after the birth of the baby, and following a religious service.

RECORDING A NAME

Recording unfamiliar names can be difficult and may lead to serious accidents. It is vital that staff are made aware of the different naming systems so that accurate information is recorded.

As the majority of Asians are not Christians, the "Christian name" has no significance. Names are given as follows:

Personal Name / Religious Name / Titular Name / Family Name.

HINDU NAMES

Hindus have a personal name, a complementary or titular name and a family name or a sub-cast name. Full names are made up of two or three parts:

Example

Personal Name	Titular Name	Family Name
LALITA VIJAY	DEVI (f) LAL (m)	SHARMA PATEL

First Name - Usually a personal name.

Middle Name - Does not stand alone. Quite often, first and second names are written as one, Lalitadevi or Vijalal.
Some common middle names:
(male)	Bhai, Chand, Das, Dev, Kant, Krishan, Parkash, Ram.
(female)	Behan, Devi, Gowri, Kumari, Lakshmi, Rani.

Family Name - Sub-cast names usually indicate the family's occupation and status. Due to the number of family members using the same name, the father's or husband's first and middle names can be used as well as the family name.

SIKH NAMES

All male Sikhs share a religious name - SINGH, which means lion, and women take the name KAUR, meaning Princess. To these names are added personal names and family names. All personal and family names are common to both men and women.

Example

Personal Name	Religious/ Titular Name	Family Name
Ravinder	Singh (m)	Sahota
Ravinder	Kaur (f)	Sahota
Baljeet	Kaur (f)	Gill
Baljeet	Singh (m)	Gill

First Name - Personal Name. Same for either sex.

Middle Name - Religious /Titular Name - Singh (m)
                                        - Kaur (f)

Family Name - Sub-cast Name, traditionally not used for religious reasons. Because of this, the name of the father or husband was used.

Ravinder Singh son of (s/o) Baljeet Singh
Baljeet Kaur wife of (w/o) Ravinder Singh.

MUSLIM NAMES

Muslim couples have different names, as do their sons and daughters. Each person has a religious or titular name, personal name and sometimes a family name. The full name is usually in two or three parts. The order of the names does not indicate whether it is a personal name or religious name. The last name is not usually a shared family name. Husband and wife could both have different family names.

Example

Mohammed	Khalid	Qureshi
Amina	Begum	Choudrey

Male
Religious Name - Mohammed
Personal Name - Khalid
Family Name - Qureshi

Female
Personal Name - Amina
Titular Name - Begum (f)
Family Name - Choudrey

Common female titular names: Bano, Begum, Sultana
Common male religious names: Mohammed, Allah, Ullah.

RECORDING ASIAN NAMES

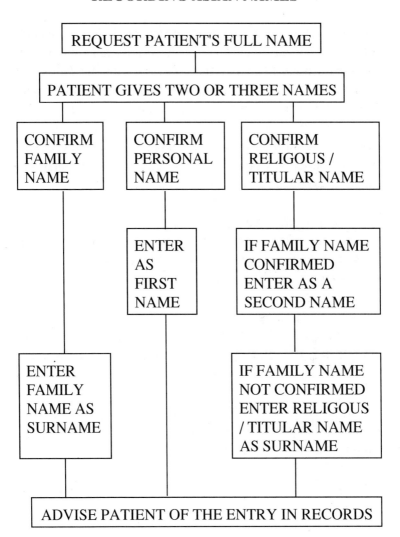

REQUEST PATIENT'S FULL NAME

PATIENT GIVES TWO OR THREE NAMES

CONFIRM FAMILY NAME

CONFIRM PERSONAL NAME

CONFIRM RELIGOUS / TITULAR NAME

ENTER AS FIRST NAME

IF FAMILY NAME CONFIRMED ENTER AS A SECOND NAME

ENTER FAMILY NAME AS SURNAME

IF FAMILY NAME NOT CONFIRMED ENTER RELIGOUS / TITULAR NAME AS SURNAME

ADVISE PATIENT OF THE ENTRY IN RECORDS

113

DIET & HEALTH

In recent times there has been an increasing interest in the subject of diet and health. Links between diseases and health are well researched and the effects of some foods on conditions such as heart disease, diabetes, obesity and hypertension are now fairly widely accepted.

Health professionals need to be aware of the dietary needs of their clients when providing care as well balanced appropriate meals assist in recovery.

In recent times many individuals are choosing to eat vegetarian meals, but they may also have personal preferences - some will eat eggs, others may eat fish and in exceptional cases they may be vegans (they will eat no animal products).

Orthodox Jews will eat only Kosher meat and Muslims will only eat Halal meat (animals slaughtered according to religious way).

Orthodox Jews, Muslims, Hindus and Sikhs will not eat foods which have come in contact with the forbidden foods, therefore the way foods are cooked and served needs to be in keeping with their religious beliefs.

The Patients Charter demands that all patients are provided with meals which take account of their religious and cultural needs.

Appended below is a brief guidance on permitted and prohibited foods according to Orthodox Jews, Hindu, Sikh and Muslim religions:

Orthodox Jews

Permitted Foods	Prohibited Foods
Fish which have fins and scales	Shellfish
Ox, Sheep, Goat, Deer	Pig
Chicken, Duck, Goose, Turkey, Pigeon, Partridge, Pheasant	Birds of Prey

N.B.

1.   Meat of birds and animals must be slaughtered and prepared to render them KOSHER.

2.   Meat and milk must be kept apart in cooking and must not be eaten in the same meal.

Hindu, Sikh and Muslim religions

Foods	Very Strict Hindus & Sikhs	Moderate Hindus & Sikhs	Liberal Hindus & Sikhs	Most Muslims
Eggs	No	Possibly	Possibly	Yes
Milk	Yes	Yes	Yes	Yes
Yoghurt	Yes	Yes	Yes	Yes
Butter/ Ghee	Yes	Yes	Yes	Yes
Cheese	Possibly	Possibly	Possibly	Possibly
Mutton	No	Possibly	Possibly	Halal
Beef	No	No	No	Halal
Pork	No	Possibly	Possibly	No
Fish	No	Possibly	Possibly	Yes
Lard	No	No	No	No

BIBLIOGRAPHY

Alexander M,
Budhwar K,
et al.

All India - A Catalogue of Everything Indian., 1986. Published by Apple Press Ltd. London.

Arora R.

Religions of the world - Sikhism, 1986. Published by Wayland Publishers Ltd. East Sussex.

Baily K.,
Blackwood A.
et al.

The Hamlyn Children's Encyclopedia in colour, 1985. Published by the Hamlyn Publishing Group Ltd, Middlesex.

Castle R. &
Weller P.

Religions in the UK. A Multi-Faith Directory, 1993. Published by the University of Derby in association with the Inter Faith Network for the United Kingdom.

Centra -
Education &
Training Services

Customs and Cultures: A Flexible Training pack, 1994. Published by Centra, Chorley, Lancashire.

Domnitz M.	Religions of the World - Judaism, 1986. Published by Wayland Publishers Ltd. East Sussex.
Eade J. & Momen R.	Bangladeshis in Britain - A National Database, 1995. Published by the Centre for Bangladeshi Studies.
National Extension College.	Caring For Everyone. Ensuring Standards of Care for Black and Ethnic Minority Patients, 1991. Produced by NEC.
Newham Health Authority Ed. Jayaratnam R.	Black & Ethnic Minorities - Cultural Awareness, 1990. Produced by Newham Health Authority, London.
Singh D. & Smith A.	The Sikh World, 1985. Published by McDonald & Co. Ltd. London.
Tames R.	Religions of the World - The Muslim World, 1982. Published by McDonald & Co. Publishers, London.

Waterside Education & Training	Promoting Equality in Care Practice, 1993. Published by The Association for Social Care Training.
Wood A.	Being a Jew 1987. Published by Acford Ltd. Chichester, Sussex.
Wood J.	Our culture - Jewish, 1988. Published by Franklin Watts, London.

NOTES